THE MINIMALIST BUDGET

MADE EASY

BY

SIMON DAVIES

Text Copyright © Simon Davies

Legal & Disclaimer

attorney, financial advisor or such other professional advisor) before using any of the suggested remedies, techniques, or information in this book.

Upon using the contents and information contained in this book, you agree to hold harmless the Author from and against any damages, costs, and expenses, including any legal fees potentially resulting from the application of any of the information provided by this book. This disclaimer applies to any loss, damages or injury caused by the use and application, whether directly or indirectly, of any advice or information presented, whether for breach of contract, tort, negligence, personal injury, criminal intent, or under any other cause of action.

You agree to accept all risks of using the information presented inside this book.

You agree that by continuing to read this book, where appropriate and/or necessary, you shall consult a professional (including but not limited to your doctor, attorney, or financial advisor or such other advisor as needed) before using any of the suggested remedies, techniques, or information in this book.

Table of Contents

INTRODUCTION

While it may come with different definitions, minimalism, for many, is a lifestyle that focuses on getting rid of the clutter in your life – both physically and mentally. Those who follow this lifestyle find that getting rid of the distractions in their lives gives them more opportunities to enjoy different aspects of life. And while minimalist lifestyle comes with many benefits, what many people enjoy the most about it is how it helps them manage their finances better.

Embracing minimalism doesn't mean that you're going to have to stop using money completely; it just means that you have to only spend money on things that can improve your life.

If you win the lottery, what would you do with the money? For most people, the first things they might think about are material things. It could be a new iPhone, a luxury car, or just anything that would make them look rich – probably to impress people who they don't even like. This wouldn't be the case for a minimalist. If a minimalist wins the lottery, he would think twice or maybe more than twice before spending his money on material things.

In this book, you will learn what a minimalist would probably buy if he wins a lottery, and even when he doesn't. You will learn where it is worth spending your money, from the perspective of a minimalist – i.e., from my perspective.

But my perception wasn't always like this.

Like many people, I used to think that money should be my number one priority as an adult. As a result, I sacrificed a lot and spent most of my life making money. I spent many hours risking my health, neglecting the people that I care about, and abandoning the things that made me genuinely happy. The more I forgot these things, the more important the money became. But even though people saw me happy and contented, I felt a lot of things were missing.

I made a good amount of money during my days in the corporate world, but ironically, that lifestyle made me spend a lot of money. And I believe that it was one of the main sources of my dissatisfaction, one that haunted me during my twenties.

When I was twenty, I worked 6 or 7 days a week, and I earned a little over $50,000 a year, which was a lot of money, considering I didn't have a degree. And again, the problem was that when I was earning 50 grand, I was spending 60 grand; the more I earned, the more I spent. Later on, I had worked my way up to a higher position, leading me to work literally 362 days a year, and I was earning in six figures. While it sounds great, I was still spending more money than I was bringing home.

So, instead of bringing home an impressive salary, I just was able to bring home anxiety, debt, and devastating amount of unhappiness. My love and hate relationship with money was, actually, my biggest root of unhappiness.

I know I deserve to be labeled as stupid. But it's not because I was wasting my hard-earned income, but because I valued it more than I should. You could say that I worshipped it.

Thanks to minimalism, however, my perspective on money has truly changed. Minimalism has helped me get rid of the excess in order for me to focus on things that are truly important. And now, at 32, I make less money than I did when I was younger. But at least I can afford everything I need, I'm not in debt, I'm don't get anxiety, and most importantly, I feel contented.

Now, when spending money on anything, I ask myself one question: *Is this worth my hard work?*

Is this shirt worth $50 of my time?
Is this meal worth $15 of my time?
Is this smartphone worth $1000 of my time?

By doing this, I can make sure that every cent I spend adds huge value to my life. I have a roof over my head, food in my stomach, clothes to keep me warm, and little things that make my life more comfortable.

Chapter 1

WHAT IS A MINIMALIST?

Before we talk about minimalist budgeting, let's talk about minimalism. Then we will discuss how it is different from the form of budgeting you're probably used to.

Again, the definition of minimalism may vary from person to person. Some people relate it to music and art, while others relate this word to architectures and interior design. I can't even find a dictionary that relates it to a lifestyle choice, so, let me define this word how I see it, as someone who is a self-proclaimed minimalist.

Minimalism is a lifestyle which involves living with only things and thoughts that are necessary for bringing happiness, health, and general well-being.

I choose to take a softer approach to a minimalist lifestyle. For me, it's more of a journey than a destination. For some, it is about living with 5 pieces of clothes or living with a minimal amount of clutter in their house.

But don't worry; minimalism is not about doing it hardcore – you don't have to reduce your possessions below a certain amount. Owning less than 50 items in your household shouldn't be your goal. Your goal is to reach the level where you are comfortable – if you want to reduce the number of your possessions, make sure that it's going to benefit you rather than make your life inconvenient.

In today's society where it's all about buying the latest fancy things, it can be a real challenge to imagine that having less stuff could be more beneficial to us. I mean, do you know anyone who would say no to a nice, big house or the latest gadgets? While there might be nothing wrong with it for some people, the fact that you're reading this might possibly mean that you've noticed how your material possessions are no longer bringing you happiness. If this is the case, then you might be ready to get more from less.

1.1 Why Less Is More

There's no denying that most of us own a great amount of excess in our lives –too much stuff, too many expenses, too many responsibilities, and too many commitments. Can you really still enjoy life despite this chaos? Do you sometimes wish you could simply push a button and turn your life around and make it more fun and relaxing? You are able to make a haven of peace not only for yourself, but you can also turn your expectations into reality. Let's bust one of the myths about minimalism – *Minimalism is all about having less stuff.*

This is the most common misconception about minimalism! Yes, for most, minimalism is about getting rid of the material things that no longer bring joy into your life, which can also deter you from moving forward.

However, minimalism is not only about material things; it could also be about having less responsibilities and fewer things to worry about. And in this subchapter, let's talk about how your schedule and responsibilities can be minimized as well.

If you do or have many things that no longer benefit or support you on a long-term basis, then getting rid of them would be a better and more beneficial choice than keeping them. But of course, it's impossible to get rid of everything – if you throw away, lessen, reduce, and remove as much as you can, you're forming a void in your life. The goal of minimalism is just to show you the truly important things in the world.

In order to understand what has to be removed and what has to be added, you can look at your activities and material things as either assets or liabilities.

Assets

An asset is something that's worth some value. If you are familiar with terms used in finance, then you know examples of assets include stocks, buildings, bonds, gold, land, etc., but we can look at assets a bit more broadly. An asset could be anything that:

- ❖ Upturns in value
- ❖ Offers something valuable like money and happiness
- ❖ Toughens and empowers you
- ❖ Takes you closer to your goals
- ❖ Offers positivity and excitement
- ❖ Calms and relaxes you
- ❖ Improves health and energy

Liabilities

Liabilities, on the other hands, are debts, obligations, and things that are worth more money than they yield. But again, let's look at it more broadly. Liability can be anything that:

- ❖ Takes from you
- ❖ Lowers in value
- ❖ Removes or lessens something valuable like money, security, joy, happiness, etc.
- ❖ Makes you weak

- ❖ Keeps you from attaining your goals
- ❖ Offers undesirable stress
- ❖ Produces anxiety or agitates
- ❖ Declines health and energy

So, in short, assets give, while liabilities take.

Now, how is this relevant to minimalism? To show you its relevance clearly, let's do a little exercise.

Make a list of all things in your life – from people that are close to you, projects you are planning to make, and all the commitments you have in your life, including expenses, goals, and belongings. Because this can be a handful task, you can make it simpler by focusing on one area first – one at a time.

List each of your responsibilities, commitments, obligations, or whatever you want to call them. If you are having a tough time remembering, you can take out a calendar and look back a few months and then carefully forward a few months to help refresh your memory. Make your list as big as you can. Your list may include random responsibilities like mowing the lawn, homeowner's association meeting, paying bills, taking dogs to the vet, volunteering, shopping for groceries, driving the kids to school, meeting your friends on weekends, etc.

Once you're done with your list, you can then categorize each of these commitments as either a LIABILITY or an ASSET. Does the responsibility or activity listed give or take? Does it help you attain the goals and dreams you have? Does it bring you joy or just stresses you out?

Now that you're done sorting them out, what you have to do next is to see if you can eliminate any of the ones listed as LIABILITY. It's impossible to get rid of all the items listed as a liability. However, still, try to get rid of as many as you can. The goal of this exercise is to make you conscious of what gives and takes, which in turn can help you make decisions about what responsibilities you can add to assets and what responsibilities you can get rid of completely.

Doing more might generate more money in your life, but ask yourself… are you really happy? Is money really more important than your happiness, health, and overall well-being? Doing less is likely to give you more: more time, more opportunities to enjoy life, and more joy.

Less Is More as Your Mantra

Integrating minimalism in every aspect of your life can bring in serenity and tranquillity. Making a space that is going to motivate you to relax and making your home a sanctuary will guarantee that will help you prioritize your needs. Similarly, focusing on activities that feed your soul and bring contentment into your life is a form of minimalism that could benefit each one of us. Following the idea behind *'less is more'* can create a haven for your home, where you are able to recharge your batteries and get yourself ready for the next day's activities while enjoying time with things you like and people you love.

1.2 Signs You Be A Minimalist In The Making

If you have been minimalizing your life or considering starting to live your life as a minimalist, then congratulations. My actions screamed minimalism long before my brain registered that I am actually trying to live as a minimalist. Read on for some tell-tale signs that you probably have the heart of a minimalist.

1. You organize all aspects of your life, and it's so therapeutic for you. You either live a laboriously tidy life or at least want to. Making lists has become a habit for you: shopping lists, to-do lists, guest lists, etc. Whenever you can see ideas and plans visibly in front of you, you feel in control, and even the hardest tasks are achievable. Presented with mess and disorder, you become disheartened.

2. You want to look presentable all the time, but you don't fuss too much over how you look. Unless it is your wedding day, you would hardly

be all dressed up. No matter what the occasion is, you'd rather wear shoes that make you feel comfortable and look natural with just enough makeup to make you feel confident.

3. In terms of clothing, you're into signature pieces that embody your personality and are made of high-quality materials – the flawlessly fitting jeans, a gorgeous couturier blazer, the classic bag. You may yield to the brief temptation of fun current trends. However, you may look at them as cheap thrills instead of investments.

4. You appreciate quality and the sophisticated things and get little to no satisfaction from lower-quality alternatives. You'd rather save up and spend $80 buying a good quality jacket, instead of buying a $30 one that is made to look exactly the same. You are attracted to fine craftsmanship and quality.

5. Wastes disgust you. Most of your makeup can last you for years, you reluctantly use up that

final centimetre of pencil, and you stubbornly excerpt 'cost for wear-out of all the pieces of clothing – which usually means getting creative with upcycling or repurposing the pieces that are no longer in style.

6. Cleanliness and functionality attract you more than the overly ornamental. So, of course, you attracted towards cleanliness, simple textures, and neutral colours.

7. You value space extremely. You'd rather have a house that has no furniture and sit on the floor like Japanese do, instead of filling all parts of your house. This doesn't mean that your home is bland or doesn't have any personality. It's actually quite far from it – since you choose all your stuff carefully, your home is a unique extension of what kind of person you are or what qualities you carry.

8. In terms of money, you're not tight with money, but at the same time, you don't spend too much

money. You would not feel hesitant to spend four digits on something you really like, but of course, you'll make sure you are getting the best quality your money can get. You love a bargain, and the % sign makes you excited.

9. Clutter is one of the things that grind your gear, so routine cleaning is something you treat as a hobby instead of a chore. Getting rid of the superfluous gives you satisfaction, as well as simplifies your life and helps you reconsider your priorities.

10. Your hatred towards clutter extends to people around you. You choose to surround yourself with those who matter most to you or those who benefit your life. So, deleting friends on Facebook who you don't connect with has become a habit for you.

Chapter 2

A Minimalist's Approach To Money

What Is Minimalist Budgeting?

Now that you probably have a better understanding as to what a minimalist is, let's now talk about what it has to do with money.

Generally, minimalism means giving value to things that are essential, while purposely getting rid of the clutter in your life. While the first thing that comes to one's mind when decluttering are material things like clothes, furniture, and other house clutter, minimalism can also be applied to your financial life.

A minimalist budget will provide you clarity on how to manage your money by decluttering your finances and putting your financial goals as your priority.

One warning that is worth mentioning, however, is that a minimalist budget does not necessarily mean you will have to spend less money. You are able to just simplify your finances while still spending a great amount of money on something that is important.

Frugality is not the same as minimalist budgeting. These two concepts are significantly different – I'll explain further in the following chapter in order for you to see what I am talking about.

However, by reducing the clutter and confusion in your financial life, you will become very aware of how you are treating your finances. By doing this, you're increasing your awareness of excessive spending. And having that awareness is the first step to changing your financial lifestyle.

2.1 What the Minimalist Budget Is Not

The minimalist budgeting will keep you from maximizing your credit card for rewards, deals, coupons, or other consumer freebies that involve subscribing to multiple accounts, which will cost you more money in the long run.

The minimalist budgeting would not save you the most dollars or turn you into the most frugal person.

Instead, the minimalist budgeting is going to help you make your finances simpler in order for you to have an easier system that helps you attain your financial objectives and in turn, makes your life easier.

I see how it made a huge difference in my life. I stopped using a credit card, which makes my life easier and more worry-free. I no longer spend money more than I have to. I have my debit card, which I use for most purchases I make. This means that I no longer benefit from the perks, bonuses, and discounts I get from using a credit card, but I don't think they are worth it, anyway. I do this for the sake of getting rid of clutter and temptation. It works for me perfectly.

Minimalist budgeting taught me the importance of sticking to what's essential in life.

It helped me and still helping me live my life in a simpler manner while still having enough money to live a comfortable life but cutting down financial responsibilities. Minimalism has made the quality of my life better not only financially but also mentally.

2.2 Minimalist Living vs. Frugal Living

Again, it's important to understand that minimalist living and frugal living are two different things.

Minimalist living is about choosing to own less stuff, while the frugal living is about spending less money on buying stuff.

By knowing the difference between the two, you will have clarity and focus on what matters the most to you, which in turn, helps you make better decisions when it comes to money.

But let's get deeper and talk about this topic further to make sure that you understand the concept behind these two things.

What is Frugal Living?

Frugal living is a lifestyle that centers on making the most of every cent you spend. It is about being thrifty with the money, like searching for the best deals and promos and using coupons or voucher codes. People who are frugal aim to spend as less money as possible.

Another quality that a frugal person usually has, unlike a minimalist, is having a lot of stuff. Most frugal individuals own a lot of stuff that they were able to acquire at a good price.

A frugal shopper: "I bought these towels at the mall today. They are of average quality, but they were on sale. Now, I have a lot more in my storage in case I'll need them later."

For many people who follow the frugal living, their argument focuses only on getting the best deal their money can get. Frugal living can bring about a lot of clutter and stuff that are not necessary for your life that you can find yourself attached to.

Now, What Is Minimalist Living?

Minimalist living, on the other hand, is a lifestyle that focuses on acquiring fewer things. People who are minimalists want to own a few but excellent-quality items that make their life better – and they don't care if they have to spend more money on them.

The goal of minimalism is how we can improve the quality of life by not owning a lot of belongings. It is about getting rid of excess and clutter and giving focus on things that don't matter.

A minimalist shopper: "I just got a new pair of gym shoes that make my training more comfortable and improve my overall performance. They're pretty expensive, but they are the only pair of gym shoes I have, so it's worth it."

I'm a minimalist at heart. I always find myself eliminating a lot of stuff I no longer need. I don't get too attached to my things anymore. The thought of having more stuff gives me anxiety. I'd rather spend more money on something that is more high-quality.

But is it possible to be both?

While there are a lot of differences between minimalism and frugality, please note that they are NOT exclusive. This means that you can be both at the same time.

The frugal-minimalist, as I call it, is the ultimate powerhouse. This person would rather spend less money when he purchases something, and at the same time, would look for the best quality his money can buy, and he also doesn't want to buy a lot. He minds the quality but would think twice before buying anything. He gives importance to his money; overspending is the last thing he would do. He also doesn't want for his house to be filled with too many things.

The frugal-minimalist is almost perfect when it comes to his spending, saving, and owning. It may be impossible to be this perfect, but we can try and fight against our natural urges, whether to spend more or own more!

2.3 How to Be More Frugal and More of A Minimalist

The lifestyle one follows vary from person to person. Now, let me share with you how I try to live as a frugal-minimalist.

To live frugally,

- ❖ Avoid buying at full price
- ❖ Buy at discount and thrift stores
- ❖ Subscribe to deal sites
- ❖ Use vouchers or coupons
- ❖ Buy second-hand
- ❖ Live below your means
- ❖ Buy in bulk
- ❖ Choose to stay at home on weekends

To live as a minimalist,

- ❖ Only buy something when you know you really need it
- ❖ Don't buy something just because it is cheap
- ❖ Always give importance to quality rather than quantity
- ❖ Learn how to let go of things when they are no longer in use
- ❖ Remove emotional attachments to material things
- ❖ Know what brings real happiness to your life

Now, you know that minimalist living and frugal living are two different mindsets. Again, the former focuses on spending less and getting the best deal but doesn't pay much attention to quality or quantity. The latter focuses on owning fewer things and living simply, with a focus on quality and not much focus on price.

You can be both minimalist and frugal. However, you may find one comes more naturally to you. Either way, both these lifestyles can help you live more intentionally and become more satisfied and happy in the long run.

2.4 Guide to Spending Money as a Minimalist

Because the idea of minimalism is living life with less in order to simplify your life, it comes with the idea of being intentional about purchasing less stuff and bringing less stuff into your home. And don't get me wrong, of course, minimalists still need to go shopping and purchase things. The idea behind learning how to shop like a minimalist is to be intentional about what you spend your money on. Being intentional with your shopping decisions lets you avoid a clutter-filled home. So, now, let me give you some strategies that will help you shop like a minimalist and encourage you to make intentional purchases.

Moderate Minimalist

If there are levels of minimalism, this is the category I fall into. But what do I mean when I say Moderate Minimalist? This is someone working hard to decrease and get rid of anything he doesn't need or love in his home. But at the same time, he's someone who is not willing to live with so little that he foregoes things that give him a convenient and comfortable life that makes him happy.

As I've said before, minimalism looks different for each of us. It is about finding a balance between too much and too little. That point of balance is anywhere that is "enough" for you. It's a place where your life is minimized and simplified to the point where you just keep the things in your home you use on a regular basis and those things make you truly happy.

Figuring out what adds Value to Your Life

For me, personally, I don't believe that to live a successfully minimalist life, you have to be restrictive on what you let yourself buy. Instead, having a minimalist mind-set and knowing how to shop like a minimalist is about being intentional with what you buy and what you bring into your home. When you find yourself at a store and see something that captures your attention, for example, a nice pair of shoes, ask yourself, do you really need it, or you're just considering buying it because you think it would look good on you? If the reason is the latter, then walk away. Shopping intentionally means prioritizing purpose over aesthetics.

We usually carefully think through our bigger purchases before making them. But it's usually the small things we buy here and there, that do not seem like a lot or don't seem like a big deal, or something that could clutter up our home. By teaching ourselves to shop like a minimalist, we can successfully live a more comfortable life and at the same time, use our money wisely.

To effectively spend money as a minimalist, I've put up a 2-part strategy that will guide you. The first part of these strategies focuses on ways to change your general mind-set and shopping behaviour to shop like a minimalist. It intends to help you become more intentional regarding what you purchase and what's your reason for buying it. On the other hand, the second part focuses on questions to ask yourself when you've decided to purchase something. These are strategies to check in with yourself and make sure that the purchase will really add value to your life.

Part 1
Different Ways to Shop Intentionally

These are ideas you can implement before you go shopping. They're general questions and strategies that are likely to change the way you buy things. These are meant to help you be deliberate and intentional with your purchases and start to shop in a minimalist manner.

This, in turn, will slow the inbound flow of clutter into your home, helping you make sure that everything you are buying and bringing into your home will be valuable and not just another addition to clutter.

1. Unsubscribe from store email lists

Getting rid of temptations is one of the best ways to avoid impulsive shopping. These businesses are advertisement champs, and they're good at what they do! It could be difficult to resist the temptation to buy when your inbox is filled with emails telling you about their promotions and latest products.

You are much more likely to make intentional purchases when you search for the item, instead of buying them just because they were offered to you.

2. Stop going to the malls and shopping centres

The same idea as controlling your email applies to this. If you spend too much time in malls or shopping places, the extremely effective marketing and advertising of the retailers will persuade you to check out their products and you might end up buying them.

If you try to avoid malls and shopping places, you can avoid the ever-effective marketing and pressure to make a purchase.

3. Research all the available options earlier

Before buying anything, search for possible options available online. Make sure to read feedback and reviews from people who have tried the product before. Look into the pros and cons of every item you want to buy.

There are times we all get captivated in the idea of needing to own something new. Doing research about it in advance can help you figure out if the item is actually something you need and if it's even worth your money.

4. Wait for the next day before purchasing

Many of us buy things in an impulse, which eventually leads to regret. In order to avoid this, you may want to wait at least 24 hours before deciding to buy the item. This will give you enough time to think if it's really worth it, or it's just going to end up being useless later.

5. Take it a step further and wait longer

If you want something that you know you don't really need but still want to buy it, then maybe stay a little bit patience and wait for a little longer. If there is something you want to buy, write it down and wait up to 30 days before buying it. If 30 days pass and you still want to buy it, then maybe you it's a wise decision to buy it.

6. Plan a no-spending day/week/month

Freezing your spending is a great way to shed some light on your spending and buying practices. This way, you cannot just save money, but you'll also have the chance to see how considerately or inconsiderately you make purchases.

7. Fairly evaluate your intentions in wanting to buy something new

Before making any purchase, honestly evaluate the reason for you for buying it in the first place. Is it because you know that it's going to add value into your life, or is it because you just want to get on with the trend? Do you just want to make yourself feel better buying something new? Are you just buying it because you want to impress people you don't even like?

Many times, many people buy something for the wrong reason. Start shopping like a minimalist by always being honest with yourself about what your motivation is for buying something.

8. Make a list and stick to it

After doing your research, have some time to think and ask yourself if you are buying for the right reasons. Make a list of what you need to buy and stick to it.

9. Pay with cash

This has been very effective for me, and I encourage everyone who wants to control their spending to do this. Instead of using a credit card or debit card, use cash. This is how your mind works -- when you pay in cash, you will be mindful and aware that the money in your pocket is already running out.

10. Choose experience over material things

If you were to choose between a brand new phone and a plane ticket to a place you haven't been before for the weekend, what would you choose? For some, it's so easy to choose the phone, arguing that it lasts for years while traveling to a new place will last for a few days. However, to live a minimalist life, you'd be encouraged to give more value to experience or something consumable to buy instead of a material thing that will just add clutter to your space.

Some examples of these experience and consumable gifts include, but are not limited to, concert tickets, lesson fees, museum passes, restaurant gift checks, groceries, etc. These are very thoughtful and personalized gifts, and more importantly, they wouldn't add clutter to your home.

11. Wear out or use up your things before replacing it

Before even considering buying something new, see first if the thing you currently have is already replaceable. This helps me drastically in eliminating the duplicates that bring clutter to your home.

12. Follow the one in, one out rule

If you want to keep your home free from clutter, this would be a great way to shop like a minimalist. This keeps clutter in check, so it does not build back in your home. Every time you bring something new into your home, look for something you may want to get rid of in place of it. Or better, look for two things you may want to get rid of in order to further lessen any clutter in your house.

Part 2

How to Buy with Intention

In this second part, we will talk about some of the important questions to ask yourself when you've finally decided to buy something. These strategies are going to help you to carefully and deliberately consider the purchase before making it, to make sure it is going to add value to your life.

1. Do you really need it?

Be honest with yourself about what you really need to buy. If the answer is not an absolute yes, then you may want to re-evaluate your decision.

2. Can you leave without it?

Again, be honest with yourself if you can go on with your life without the item you are considering to buy. There are times we can get very excited about the idea of owning something new. Or settle for something that's not really worth it just because we want something new. If you know you can get by without it, or it's not an inconvenience not owning it, then maybe ditch it.

3. Where are you going to put the item?

In order to avoid more clutter, one of the best solutions you will have is to find a place for them. Finding a place where things can easily be accessed is necessary to keep them from turning into clutter. If you can't think of any place to put the items after buying them, then hold off buying them until you get a place or space in your house where you can put them.

4. How often will you use them?

How essential the item is in your daily life? If you'll use it often and it is going to add value to your life while you're doing it, then it's probably worth your money. On the other hand, if it is something you're only going to use sometimes, then leave it. Not to mention, if you buy it, you will have to keep it, maintain it, and clean it, but you would not actually use it frequently.

5. Do you already have something that you can use instead?

With your creativity and wit, you might see that you already have something you could use instead of the item you want to buy.

Whether it is a piece of garment or a kitchen gadget, if you already have something similar or something that serves the same purpose you are looking for, you might not have to buy something new after all.

6. **What's something you're willing to let go in replacement of something you are planning to buy?**

Remember the one in, one out rule I mentioned earlier? You must choose what you are willing to get rid of for the new item you are planning to buy.

And remember to always stick to this rule. After buying, get rid of the item you are willing to let go and either throw it away, donate it, or sell it.

2.5 Intention over Restriction

I'm not saying that you cannot have any fun shopping or ever treat yourself to buy something new. It isn't about restricting yourself to the point that it makes you feel stressed out and unhappy.

Actually, it is supposed to give you the opposite effect! Again, the point of learning how to shop like a minimalist is to become more intentional with the things you buy and bring into your household, to avoid cluttering your home and space with stuff that is not adding value to your life. The goal is to give yourself more space, time, and freedom to live life to the fullest and to enable you to live a life filled with the most important things: the people you truly care about.

I know that it might not always be "fun" to say no to buying more or getting the latest stuff. However, learning to shop like a minimalist is surely going to recompense in the long run when you realize that your home is uncluttered and very liveable. When you're not spending your free time organizing and cleaning the things you own, instead of doing something else more important, then you will get the reward for a minimalistic life.

The intentional shopping choices you make right now will let you spend your weekend afternoons doing something you enjoy and love instead of cleaning your whole house over and over again.

Again, as I said earlier, everyone, including serious minimalists, need to buy new things from time to time.

Things get worn out and broken and might need a replacement. However, when you know how to shop like a minimalist and how to embrace a minimalist mind-set, you will also know the difference between buying things mindlessly and buying something that is truly worth it. And purchasing things after careful consideration and making a thoughtful decision to buy derived from the value is going add value to your life.

2.6 The 50/30/20 Rule of Budgeting

Budgeting is not only about having enough money to pay your bills and being able to pay them on time – budgeting should about determine how much you must be spending and on what. The 50/20/30 rule of budgeting is a comparative guideline that is able to help you keep your spending in alliance with your savings goals.

Adults are able to benefit significantly from following the simple ideologies set forth by this rule of budgeting. As long as you know how to attain a stable budget, you are able to take the next steps to further modify this rule around your own unique goals and expenses.

The 50/20/30 budgeting rule can particularly help young adults who are starting to deal with the tricky world of finance. By making an effort of getting into this system, budgeting, in general, would be an easy thing for you to deal with. Of course, you can always make adjustments based on your lifestyle and preferences. However, by keeping yourself close to the core idea of this budgeting system, you are guaranteed to gain financial ground, instead of losing it.

50% of Your Income – Essentials

To start following this rule, allocate no more than half of your income for the absolute necessities in your life. This might seem like a high fraction of your income, but when you consider all things that fall into this category, it starts to make a little more sense.

To make it clear, what I mean by essential expenses are those ones you'd almost definitely need to pay, no matter where you are living, where you are working, or what your goals are. Generally, these expenses are almost the same for everybody and include housing, food, transportation expenses, and of course, the utility bills. The fraction allows you to adjust, while still keeping a comprehensive, stable budget. And keep in mind that it is more about the total amount compared to individual costs. For example, some people are living in high-rent areas, yet are able to walk to work; similarly, others benefit from much lower housing expenses while dealing with more expensive transportation fee.

20% of Your Income – Savings

The following step is to bestow 20% of your take-home income toward savings. This includes debt payments, savings plans, and rainy-day funds – things you must add to, but which would not imperil your life or make you homeless if you did not. That is a bit of a generalization, but you get the idea. This class of expenses must only be paid after your essentials are already covered and before you even consider anything in the following category.

You can look at it as your "get ahead" category. Whereas 50% of your income is the goal for essentials, 20% – or more – must be your goal in terms of obligations. You will be able to pay off your debt faster and make more important steps toward a stress-free future by dedicating as much of your income as you can to this category.

The word "retirement" may not bring a sense of urgency when you are only in your early 20s. However, it surely will become more persistent in many years to come. Just remember that the advantage of starting while you are young is that you'll earn bigger interest the longer you allow the funds to grow.

30% of Your Income – Personal Expenses

Now, to the last category, and it is also the one that can truly make the most difference in your budget are the personal expenses you make. There are financial experts that consider this category totally optional. However, in today's world, a lot of these so-called luxuries have taken on more of an obligatory position. It all depends on what your goal in life is and what you are willing to sacrifice. The reason that this category takes a bigger fraction compared to the previous category is due to the reason that a lot of things falls into it.

These personal expenses include things like your mobile phone plan, internet bill, and trips. If you're travel expansively or work online, your mobile internet plan is possibly more of a necessity and not a luxury. But you need some wiggle room because you can choose which plan to pay for. Other things in this category include coffee shop visits, gym memberships, evenings with friends, and the like. You're the only one who can choose which of your expenses can be labelled as "personal," and which ones are really obligatory. The same as how no more than 50 % of your income must go toward vital expenses, 30% is the maximum amount you may spend on personal needs. The fewer expenses you have in this category, the more development you will make settling down your debt and working hard towards your goals.

Creating good habits will pay off in the long term. You're not required to have a high income to follow the creeds of the 50/20/30 budgeting rule; anybody can do it. Because this is a percentage-based system, similar amounts apply whether you are earning an entry-level salary and earning handsome amount of money, or if you have been working for years and have a lot of sources of income.

There's something you need to remember, though: You don't have to take this rule literally. While the proportions are sound, our lives vary from person to person. This plan does provide an outline for you to work within. When you review your income and spending and define what's important and what is not, only then you are able to make a budget that helps you make the most of your income. Many years from now, you are still able to fall back on the same guidelines to assist you with your budget as your life evolves.

Chapter 3

AVOIDING UNNECESSARY SPENDING

3.1 The Psychology of Spending Money

The purpose and importance of money may vary from person to person. The way you look at money has a direct influence on what you currently have in your life and is going to be a determining factor of how much you'll inevitably draw to your life.

Why do people spend too much and why for many, curbing those impulses can be too difficult? Even though it looks simple from the outside, the truth is, the reasons behind people's spending can be rather complicated. A lot of research has shown that. Below I listed some of the main reasons that trigger people to spend and overspend.

Emotional triggers

It's human nature to want things; these wants include health, happiness, being loved, safety, and to get those things better than others. Many companies use advertising strategies that make people want to have better things than others. Alternatively, they trigger fear when selling products that claim to make your home more secure, make you safe from accidents, and prevent your body from changing negatively. Marketers study the lifestyles of the consumers and their world views to address specific psychological triggers. When successfully tapped, it's going to be hard to remain rational in the face of them.

People love a bargain

Seeing something at a reduced price makes people feel like they are smart consumers. However, it could counter your goal when you had not planned on making buying that anyway, had not yet budgeted for it, or had not planned on that much money on anything anyway!

Too many options

The more decisions you need to make, the less likely it is for you to fight temptation. According to multiple types of research, when the willpower of a person is run down, they tend to spend more money and buy more items than those who have not recently used their willpower.

According to the American Psychological Society, willpower can be compared to a muscle that gets tired after being used for a certain period. Those who are financially insecure and thus always facing hard financial decisions are at a greater risk of exhausting willpower. According to one study, for example, people who are not financially secure are more likely to purchase food and drink while shopping compared to people who are well off. There are also studies that have shown shoppers in malls are likely to make most of their purchases in the third hour of their time there.

In other words, when our willpower is exhausted, we're more likely to be persuaded by urges, desires, and cravings—even though we may regret those purchases later on.

Needs versus wants

The result of globalized trade is that the products that were used to be seen as luxury items – for example, electronics and toys – are now increasingly produced in bulk. This explosion of consumer goods has made products cheaper and less valuable. A profusion of affordable things isn't essentially a bad thing. However, it's important to know whether something is a need or a want.

Buying love

Special occasions like birthdays, Christmas Day, and anniversaries are traditional reasons to give gifts. Actually, spending during the winter holidays makes up 20% of total annual retail sales in America. Similarly, Mother's Day, Valentine's Day, Father's Day, Graduation Day, and the like, have presented themselves as reasons to give, and of course, spend money. If you associate your appreciation with the price of your gift, you're more likely to spend too much. In a world that is too materialistic, it's easy to forget how experiences and memories are far more valuable than material things.

Filling a void

Based on the research done by the University of Michigan's Ross School of Business in 2014, shopping helps people feel better. As people feel sad or deserted about a situation they've found themselves in, they claim, "retail therapy," may help people feel better. That's for the reason that the options involved in shopping can boost their sense of personal control. Shopping, just like drinking alcohol and overeating, can help some people manage their stress.

Quick thrills

Also known as "present bias," sellers take advantage of the fact that the charm of getting something today is stronger compared to the appeal of getting something later on. But of course, the problem is that instant gratification can get in the way of a person's long-term goals, even though the latter would give far more happiness in the long run. Furthermore, credit cards and online shopping have made instant gratification easier to gain more than ever.

Marketers are fully aware of the powers that influence the behaviour of consumers. As those forces hit your deepest emotions, including your dreams and fears, you can easily fall victim to at least a few of what's mentioned above.

But fortunately, the more you are aware of these forces and how they approach you, the easier it is going to be for you to deal with these changes.

It's important to think in abundance and accept that you already have enough for what you need. The key ingredient to changing the way you think of money from a harmful mind-set to a positive mind-set is to make yourself aware of the words you use. Never call yourself broke to describe your personal financial situation; instead, use tight budget or fixed income. The more you use different words of abundance to classify your situation, the more your subconscious will think that those words are true.

3.2 How to Differentiate Compulsive from Excessive Spending

You get your pay check, and you're very thrilled about it. You've planned on saving half of it in your bank account. But instead, you clicked on a little banner on your browser showing pictures of shoes you think would look good on you. You put them in your cart, and as you're browsing on the site, you saw a bag that is on sale. You put it in your cart as well thinking that if you buy it later, it might already be gone and by buying it now, you can save on shipping fee. Now you have a nice pair of shoes and a bag. You continue buying stuff even though you already have a lot of it and you will barely use the new ones and obviously, you're on the verge of reaching your credit card's maximum limit. A part of you is already panicking, but you still keep buying.

Well, I have news for you: you're a compulsive spender. This is a form of addiction that is more commonly observed in women than in men. Women can easily spend their whole pay check in one store.

There are several possible reasons for compulsive spending, and some of those reasons are temporary depression or loneliness. Some people think that compulsive spending can make them feel happy or contented, but this is not always the case. This is because even though compulsive spending gives brief pleasure, it could just actually makes your life worse.

After spending most, if not all, of your money, you might face an emergency, and you'll be left without financial help. To a great extent, it cannot only affect you, but also your family, your health, and even your job as you're always dealing with the pressure of how you're going to cope your expenses and pay bills and other things that involve financial settlement. You might have to take an extra job to settle the bills, which may impede your credit scores.

Yes, you might not be taking drugs or drinking a lot of alcohol – you're just shopping… too much. However, this extreme spending is considered as addiction, and you might have a compulsive spending disorder. It's a disorder that's completely destroying you much faster than you'd ever think of.

A compulsive spending disorder triggers you to spend more and more money on things – even if it's beyond your capacity or it's something you don't actually need. The compulsive spending disorder is a symptom that indicates that someone is extremely disturbed. Recognizing and acknowledging that you have a problem is the best way to overcome it. If you know that your compulsive spending is the reason for your problems, it is going to be easier for you to avoid it. You can always talk to a therapist. You are able to overcome the compulsive spending disorder because this ever-addictive behaviour can be treated. With some help, you can overcome this disorder.

3.3 Effective Ways to Overcome Overspending

You might be thinking that recognizing excessive personal spending is easy – when someone is shopping for many things without caring about the bill. This observation might be true, but is a threat of passing judgment, and maybe not having enough details about the person being seen. To identify that a person overspends, you need to see first his goal for buying too many things. Judging someone from another's person's perspective is not easy, but seeing it in yourself and identifying if you are overspending is easier. If you believe that you tend to overspend, then this is for you. Below is a basic plan that can immediately help you to regulate excessive spending.

1. Create a future reference by visualizing your anticipated position 3 to 5 years from now. It's a great idea to create a long-term position first before thinking of short-term to help you remain focused and more motivated.

2. List down your visualization with a header "Vision Statement" and add a projected emotional response as you trip towards fulfilment.

3. Write an achievement goal that's important to help you understand your vision in each of the following areas like social, educational, financial, and personal health.

4. Plan the dollar amount that is going to be necessary to achieve your goals and see your vision in 3 to 5 years.

5. Define your current spending pattern per month in order to see if you'll have the resources or if you'll need to make changes in order to see your vision in the following years.

This step by step method will help you in self-evaluation and determine your spending pattern. This will give you information to help you decide if you're spending excessively.

A lot of people see personal budget planning from a negative perspective. They see it either as a frantic attempt to avoid debt or some sort of handcuffs that prevent them from enjoying things that they want.

By looking at it this way, following a budget is only a necessary evil. However, it may be more helpful to focus on the long-term benefits that can come from the traditional budgeting process like composure and eventually, financial freedom.

Let's be honest. Most of us would rather spend as much money as we want without any limitations. It's in our nature to desire more for ourselves. Unfortunately, not all of us have infinite resources. So, choices are necessary.

3.4 Importance of Budgeting

Instead of tying us down, the act of making a personal budget is essentially a liberating exercise. It lets us make rational selections when it comes to our spending as we consider our entire financial picture. Incautious spending impulsively is traded by process of logical decision-making. It lets us prioritize our needs and desires in both short term and long term.

Without a budget, the money we worked hard for will have a tendency to go down the drain. A lot of people have a problem understanding why they don't have money left at the end of the month. Astonishingly, this happens not only to those who have low-paying jobs but also to those who have high-paying jobs.

If you're one of the people whose pay check doesn't stretch to cover each of your expenses, try to keep track of your spending for a month. Make sure you keep a record of everything you spend, whether by cash, credit cards, or check. You might be surprised how much money you spend on small purchases without having a second thought.

Extra Money for Long-Term Goals

Even more astounding is what you are able to save if you choose to get rid of those small, unnecessary purchases. If you take the money you'd have spent every month and put it toward settling your debt, you might be able to significantly lessen your number of payments along with the total amount of interest you need to pay.

Similarly, if your debts are settled and you want to save a bit of extra every month, you build up a considerable amount. For example, let's say you could save $100 every month by not having your coffee. If you were to invest that cash at a conservative 4% interest rate for more than a 40-year working career, you'd have more than $118,000!

This is only one example. When you look closely at how you spend, you might be able to find a lot of unnecessary expenses to get rid of.

By planning your personal budget, you are able to take control of your financial situation, instead of letting it control you. You are able to be in a place to substitute your instant gratification with the help of financial goals that need some time to achieve. Then, you are able to truly experience life without having to worry about your financial situation.

Learning *how to control spending and the use of credit cards* will mean the need to understand why you spend.

If you are aware of the emotional reasons behind your spending, resisting it would be easier.

While the occasional shopping spree might seem harmless, the problem is that the effect of spending is so easy to underestimate. And, unfortunately, using words like 'shopaholics' makes it sound like it's a fun activity you can be proud of. But the effects hit you hard.

This spending indulgence normally comes with the use of using credit cards. It's a lot easier to give out the plastic and not dwell on what you're spending. What you have to know is that credit cards are essentially a loan that has to be repaid, and you'll pay interest on your loan balance.

You can take control of your use of credit card using the following steps:

❖ Plan your budget, taking note of all of your essential expenses like housing expenses, meals, and loan payments. Add other living expenses and subtract them from your income. You must know what's coming in and what's going out in order to know which changes you need to make. You need to be very honest with yourself.

❖ Add a credit card payment in your budget. This has   to be more   than   the minimum obligatory.

❖ Have a notebook where you can record all of your spending you do for a couple of months regardless of how small the purchase. You will be amazed at how much you put out.

❖ When you go out, you may want to leave your card at home. Ask a reliable friend to keep it for you to control your spending.

❖ Choose to use cash. Think that if you don't have cash, then it means you can't afford it.

❖ Before you spend anything, make sure to think twice. Ask yourself if you need that item. Don't buy things impulsively, try to sleep on it.

Budgeting and emotions come hand in hand, so by controlling one of them, you are also affecting the other.

Chapter 4

CREATING AN EFFECTIVE BUDGET

Whatever you are looking for in life, whether it is wealth, health, prosperity, love, or just success along the way, everything begins with your mind-set.

But can you even change the way you look at money? There are different tactics on how you are able to change your mind-set.

Our mind is extremely powerful, and when used the right way, you are able to change your life around. Keep reading to know how you can alter your perspective on the money with the following simple to follow steps.

Why Is It Important To Change The Way You See Money?

I grew up in a family that was struggling with money. Looking back, I blame my parents for having "just enough" to survive. Because their mind was set to: "as long as you have enough to get by, it's enough."

But I need to blame myself more for accepting this mind-set from them.

Of course, there are a lot of people out there who'd be very happy with having enough money to survive, especially the ones who live pay check by pay check. Having such a narrow perspective on money or about the abundance of money could hold you back in your life.

Try to look at it this way: having enough money is going to get you the absolute minimum. It may perhaps...

...settle the bills but not give you enough money to set aside.

...buy your meals, but not the pleasure of letting you try new dishes, eating out, or choosing healthier options.

...let you work very hard for your money but making you sacrifice time and passion.

…give you the chance to have occasional vacation but with limited funds and not enjoying the luxury of business class and 5-star hotels.

…make you survive but not entirely experience life.

You see, having enough can make you survive, but it wouldn't let you enjoy life to the fullest. This is going to cost money, and I believe that every one of us deserves to live our life the way we want.

That was one of the main reasons I felt unhappy and looked for something until my mind-set towards money changed. I was able to change it. And so can everyone!

Most people think that having the right mind-set is something you might or might not have; they think that it is something someone is born with, but that's not really the case. It is something you are able to learn and train, just like any skills or talent one could have. Here are some ways to train yourself to improve your relationship with money.

1. Forget all the things you learned as a kid

Well, I'm not talking literally everything, but in terms of our belief system, most of us have unfortunately usually gotten a completely wrong message.

I'm sure; as a kid, you heard an adult saying, "Money doesn't grow on trees."

Well, turns out I was not the cleverest kid; otherwise, I'd have told them that money actually grows on trees because they are used to make paper.

But that's not the point! The point is I believe that people like to use sayings like this too casually and don't really consider how damaging they could be to a young person's mind.

So, if you have kids who are too young to understand deep sayings or idioms, try not to use them. You can explain things better in simple words rather than confusing them.

2. Forget about your past

It's not just what others told you regarding money, but it's also about what belief system you made yourself.

I told you earlier how I unhappy I was in the past even though I earned a handsome amount of money. And if I were living the same way right now, I wouldn't be here in my situation right now. I wouldn't be where I wanted to be.

For example, I lost a lot of money on a business that failed many years back. It took me quite a while before I was able to recover. If I let it become my "new reality" – that I would just lose a lot of money if I start a business again, then I would not have a successful business at present.

Don't let your past define what you are now and what you could do in the future. One can always learn from his mistakes and can turn everything around if he wants it enough.

So, learn from your past, once you are done, leave it all behind and start a new chapter.

3. Change your money story

Forgetting something bad from the past might not be too difficult, but how about your present struggles?

If you're currently dealing with debts or in a situation that involves money, it's even more important to change your feelings about this immediately. It's going to be difficult to attract abundance and positivity when you're in a state of lacking.

But the good news is that you can trick your mind into the state of abundance, no matter what kind of situation you are in at present.

I'm not suggesting that you should maximize your credit card to afford to live in luxury even if you are about to lose your car.

But in case you don't have any debt you need to pay off, then why not?

What I'm saying is that don't live off the idea that you can't afford the good things when you know you could.

Don't deprive yourself of the good things because you love money to the point that you don't want to spend it anymore.

Ask yourself – do you live to work, or do you work to live? Don't be afraid to spend your money on things that matter. This being said, you must still be careful about where you spend your money. A minimalist budgeter is not afraid to spend his money, but rather, afraid to spend his money on things that wouldn't bring him joy or improve his life in the long run.

4. Fake it until you make it

Once you got over the first three points, you can now proceed to talk to others regarding your situation as if.

I'm encouraging you to lie; in fact, please don't! You can just say something like, "I have a stable money situation right now; I'm aiming to work on my money mind-set, though."

What I meant by "fake it until you make it", is to make yourself believe the positive side all the time, even if it means you're not really confident with your money situation.

When you start telling your goals to people, you will be more motivated to prove to them that you are telling the truth. But please, don't put yourself in a situation where you will find yourself hanging by a thread. For example, although it might be your dream to buy a beach property on an isolated island, you don't have to tell them that you are already buying that property when you are not yet.

Always believe in your dreams and make them happen.

5. Make a vision board

When changing your mind-set, visualization is such an effective tool, and a vision board could absolutely help you throughout the process.

When you start taking advantage of a vision board, you would be amazed at how powerful the law of attraction is when it comes to changing your perceptions towards money.

On your vision board, start putting the amount of money you wanted to earn, you can change it as your earning shows signs of progress. And when you look back, you will see how the number changes over time.

This might sound very simple, but it could truly make a great change in your life.

6. Practice gratitude

What are the things you are thankful for?

Create a gratitude list or a journal and list down the things that make you happy on a daily basis. This method will show you the magic of the law of attraction.

At the end of the day, I write everything I am thankful for on that day, and it makes me realize how lucky I am for having my life. This exercise improves your overall mind-set and not just your mind-set towards money.

Try it out, and you will immediately see what I am talking about. Some people do this in the morning, while for me – like I said – I do this before I go to bed.

However, practicing gratitude is a lot more than simply writing down the things that make you thankful. Gratitude is something you must live the whole of your day, no actually your whole life.

You can start by being grateful for all the small things you have in your life, and I am 100% sure that no matter what situation you are in at the moment, once you start working on your gratitude, you'll find more and more things you will be happy about.

It's not going to take long until you realize that this is going to change your whole mind-set; your filter is going to be set to things you're grateful for, and you'll attract more good things.

7. Start to love money (but not too much)

Okay, this one should not be too difficult. But because this is something that is very important, I should add it to the list.

There's no way you can build a positive money mind-set if you have any negative feelings towards money.

There's nothing bad with being wealthy – in fact, it's a good thing!

I don't believe that money is the root of evil. It is the person who holds the money who is accountable for the evil things that are taking place! Some people look at money as power – power that they can use to general good things and bad things.

But money is not the culprit.

I mean, just think about the things money can do to improve people's lives.

Don't feel guilty for loving money. If you feel a little bit uncomfortable for having a lot of money while some people are living in poverty, then you can always help them.

You can always help people through charities.

Doing this will not only make them happy, but the sense of fulfilment knowing that you offered a good deed would make you so much proud of yourself.

So, if ever you have negative feelings towards money, try to turn them around, and think of all the good things you could do with it.

8. Be more confident

Many people underestimate what they are worth. But what they don't know is that it's one of the worst things they could do to themselves.

Everyone always has something to offer, and it's important for each one of us to focus on those things.

This could be raising the rate for your products or services or asking for a salary raise from your boss.

Never sell yourself short – you'll immediately realize that you're worth a lot and you deserve more than you are actually getting. You must be confident your time and skills are worth the money you want to have.

9. Set your goals high

The problem with some goals is that they're not big enough to keep you motivated to work on them.

Big goals can truly fire you up. So, in terms of money, it is even more essential that you're thinking big.

No matter what you can offer in the world to earn money in return, I'm sure that there's someone in the world doing the same and earning a lot more money than you can ever imagine.

I mean in today's world, it's almost normal to hear people doing these following things while earning a handsome amount of money:

- ❖ Helping people in need
- ❖ Traveling the world
- ❖ Sleeping
- ❖ Tasting food
- ❖ Staying at home

So don't you think it is time to think big and change how you see money?

Of course, there are more things you can do to change your mind-set from dearth to abundance. It's just all up to you how you can go about it. But I hope the tips are enough to help you get started without your shift.

4.1 7 Ways to Save Money with Minimalism

After finishing grad school, I was a complete mess. In debt and confused, you can compare my life as if I was climbing a mountain of problems without a clear vision of where it is going to end. Fortunately, I since have found a minimalist lifestyle. It allowed me to save money and create a plan on how I am should deal with my debt. Now, let me talk about the ways I used to save money through minimalism.

1. I fixed my hobbies

We live in a time where almost every possible hobby or pastime is within our reach. Gone are the days we need to drive to the nearest theater or rent tapes and CDs if we want to watch movies. We can literally browse hundreds of movies and watch them through our computer or even a smartphone.

For me, however, this excess of choice led to infinite indecision. There are too many options. Choosing has been a challenge. So, not only I wasted money paying for subscriptions, but I also wasted my time.

I thought hard about what hobbies I want to try and lock in the things that I truly enjoyed spending time on. I also tried looking for more activities that wouldn't require me to spend money. Some of those hobbies include riding my bike and hiking.

2. I consolidated my pantry

Same as the aforementioned situation, I had an ever-changing interest in different kinds of foods. I was not quite at the point where I was eating instant noodles every night, but I certainly had to watch my meal budget. What I did that certainly helped me the most was coming up with a weekly meal plan.

On Sunday evening, I would prepare a full set of meals for lunch, snack, and dinner. I normally used cheap ingredients like pasta or rice, and making tasty and healthy dishes with a great range of vegetables has saved me a lot of money.

I also saved tons of money by growing my own supply of some items that could be expensive. Basil, for example – a bottle of basil that I need to make 4 servings of pesto used to cost me $5. Sometimes I would not even use the entire container before it went bad. This spring, I planted basil plants together with some other herbs for about $10, which gives me enough for the whole summer.

3. I used fewer appliances

Many people I know have two or more refrigerators in their home. Some keep a lot of frozen food and such, which is understandable. However, there are others who simply need space for a great range of snacks and desserts.

My sister even kept two washers around just for the reason that for her, moving heavy things is so inconvenient. That's when I saw several problems with that. Not just do old appliances consume a lot of space, things like old refrigerators could have chemicals in them that could seriously harm the environment and even humans if not disposed of properly.

4. I tried thinking smaller

For me, this step came a little later in the process, and it makes sense that it did. When I came to a point where I had so many kitchen gadgets, a lot of hobbies, as well as wasteful appliances, I tried to convince myself that I needed a huge house in order for me to have enough room for everything I had.

But ironically, the moment I cleared up other parts of my life, I was more eager to move to a smaller space. And as I mentioned earlier, this also had a surprising effect on keeping me honest in my minimalist lifestyle. I control my impulse purchases with one question, "Am I going to have a space for this?"

5. I used my credit card carefully

I know how the use of a credit card is very convenient. I'm not going to tell you to stop using it completely. In fact, I did not even get rid of mine, and there have been times when it saved me from trouble due to its convenience.

Now, just focus on "used it carefully". This just means you have to be responsible every time you use it. I used it only during the times I REALLY needed it.

6. I changed my mindset

Every practical advice in the world will not help you if you do not adopt a great mindset. Today, I try to focus on the good things that I can do for myself and for others, and I mainly do it by decluttering. I have a basket in my garage where I put everything that I no longer want or need. I was able to get rid of a lot of clutter by doing this. I donated them, sold them, or just disposed them.

I know that from the outside, minimalist budgeting or lifestyle itself may look like a weird cult for others – I used to look at it this way. It included people who were not like me at all. I thought it minimalists are individuals who can easily give up and let go of a lot of things in their life that I couldn't even imagine doing back then. I have since learned that this is not the case at all, obviously. For me, a minimalist lifestyle is fueled by lifestyle changes and gentle attitude, by dealing with problems one by one with a positive and generous mindset.

4.2 Steps to Having an Effective Minimalist Budget

For many people, finance can be truly complicated… but the truth is, it doesn't have to be. With a bit of effort, you are able to simplify your financial life and eliminate all the financial headaches you might be facing.

I consider myself a minimalist, and that's why I try to shy from any forms of complexities. I try to do everything in the simplest way possible. I go for stress-free solutions – I try to do things simpler so I can focus on more important things in my life.

Now, let's talk about how I simplify my financial life.

I'm going to share with you a step-by-step guide on how I made a practical budget that helped me reach my financial goals. "Practical" would be the keyword here.

If you have soaring hopes, just like when I started budgeting, and you make your budget too restrictive, it's likely for you to be unsuccessful in this. What's worse is that you might begin to have a mentality that you are just not great with money. This is not true at all. Every single one of us can be smart with their money. I truly believe that money management has a lot to do about having the right combination of mind-set and knowledge. You are required to have knowledge in order to make a plan that makes your money work for you, and at the same time, you need the mind-set to effectively follow-through with your plan.

I haven't met any person who has reached their financial goals without any type of budgeting system. A budget is probably the most important step towards financial freedom and success. There are a lot of different ways to budget. Some would do bi-monthly budgeting, others would do monthly budgeting, and there are some who would even do it annually.

It's important for you to find what really works for you. This might be dependent on three different factors: your salary schedule, your regular spending, and what triggers your spending. If shopping has become your weakness when you're feeling stressed out, having a monthly budget instead of an annual budget will be ideal for you.

In my case, I get paid every 15 days, have to settle a couple of major expenses, and my weakness is night outs with my friends. I find that making a monthly budget worked best for me.

At first, I followed the bi-monthly budgeting. It was so difficult for me, and unsurprisingly, I failed to keep my expenses within my set budget. How did this happen, you may ask...

Well, let me give you an example of why. Okay, so I gave myself $80.00 for when I go out with my friends. Well, technically I gave myself $160.00 per month for when I go out with my friends, but since I split my month into two budgets, I had no flexibility with that spending.

Now, let's get into it – Here are the steps I took to deal with my current budget, which works very well for me, that I want to share with you in the hope that they help you with your own budget planning.

Step 1: Track Your Spending Every Day for a Month

It's so easy to find tips and advice online that suggests how you can track your spending for 3 months before creating a budget. However, if you are reading this, I'd be guessing that you probably don't want to wait three more months to start changing your budget. If you're really serious about generating a realistic budget, you can start tracking your spending right now. It doesn't matter if it's in this middle of the month – simply record all your expenses for the following 30 days and then begin your budget at the beginning of next month.

You can get a journal, but I just like using the simple "Notes" App on my smartphone to track all the things I need to document. Because I almost always have my phone with me, I simply fill this in whenever I have to spend money on something. If I'm in a rush, I would simply ask for a receipt or check my bank account to record them at the end of the day.

I like putting things in categories. I suggest that when you are tracking your daily spending before making your first budget, you may want to put your expenses in categories as well. It is easier to figure out what your categories will look like when all things are already sorted. For example, try not to put, "burger—$5.00." Instead, you may want to write "eating out—$5.00." It is going to make things a lot easier by the time you need to calculate your expenses.

If you are going to make a monthly budget, you may want to up your spending around two weeks into your budget tracking. If you think you are spending too much on something, then try to lessen that spending in the following weeks. By following this, you will have you a better sense of what expenses you can realistically reduce when you are making your first budget.

Since I make monthly budgets, I compute my spending in every category in the middle of the month. I am able to determine precisely what spending money I have left in every category I listed. I normally then write something very informal:

"As of March 15:
Groceries—$100
Transport—$90
Entertainment—$80
...."

I have this information in my smartphone, again normally within the same note, so that I can easily look at it before I buy something.

Because I have gotten used to tracking my spending, it has become very easy for me. When it becomes a habit, it would literally take 5 seconds for you to take out your phone and write the information you need. It also literally takes not more than 10 minutes to review the categories.

Step 2: Know Your Fixed Spending

Your fixed spending is the expenses that you have to settle on a regular basis, usually every month. The items in this category include, but are not limited to the following:

- ❖ Rent

- ❖ Electricity

- ❖ Water

- ❖ Mobile

- ❖ Retirement Savings

As the minimum payment on your student loans is going to change as you are paying off your dues, you must eventually have an estimate as to what it is going to be.

Say, for example, the minimum payment last month was $250.00. Instead, you can make the minimum payment amount for your student loans $350.00. That way, in case it changes, you know you can cover it. But then again, you can simply check your student loan balance by the end of the month to identify the minimum payment before finalizing the budget for the following month.

Your phone bill might also occasionally vary. There might be some months when you could unintentionally go beyond your data limit and have to pay more the following month. It is not really a big deal, but you have to remember that when you are making the budget for next month.

While these are considered as "fixed" spending, you still need to make a budget for every single month. And even though you can normally just copy and paste these expenses when planning your budget next month, it's still important to go over each item, just to make sure.

Other things you may want to include under fixed spending are:

- ❖ Utilities
- ❖ Car Insurance
- ❖ Subscriptions (i.e., gym membership, Netflix)
- ❖ Insurance
- ❖ House maintenance
- ❖ The minimum payment for loans and debts

Step 3: Make Yourself Aware of Your Variable Expenses

These are expenses that you, usually, have more discretion over.

Here are some of the examples:

- ❖ Dining Out
- ❖ Coffee

- ❖ Groceries

- ❖ Entertainment

- ❖ Pet Supplies

- ❖ Transportation

- ❖ Healthcare

- ❖ Gifts

- ❖ Miscellaneous Fund

My category for grocery hasn't been changed for months. I usually change it when there are occasions when I have to prepare more food than the usual, like Christmas day, birthdays, etc.

"Personal Funds" are the funds I can use for personal expenses. I use this category when I have to pay for books, clothes, medicine, and anything I feel like treating myself with. Furthermore, if I have maxed out the budget for other categories, and I manage to have some left in this category, I would use this budget.

I find having a "Miscellaneous Fund" extremely important. This is basically an emergency fund for unexpected expenses. You never know what might happen! Although the following a strict budget is doable, there are still instances where you have no choice but to spend outside your planned budget categories.

Some of the things you might need this budget for are the following:

Car or Home Maintenance

Gifts for a special occasion

Someone has to borrow money

Unplanned donation

Step 4: Choose What to Do with What's Left

Okay, now it's time for you to do some basic math. Deduct the total amount of your fixed spending and variable expenses from your monthly net income and presto! That is the amount of money you are left with. Keep in mind that these remainders shouldn't be used to satisfy your leisure. Don't go spend them at a fancy restaurant or to watch a movie.

This money must strictly be used to support your bigger financial goals. You could add that money to the next month's emergency fund, or you could simply save it.

If you have debts to settle, then your number one priority to achieve financial freedom is to pay them off.

Also, if you have different goals like moving to a new house, a dream vacation, saving for a wedding, then you are able to use your discretion on how to split up this money. But then again, using this money on different random things can be a great mistake.

Step 5: Track Your Spending... Again

You are not done just yet!

You're probably wondering why I am telling you to track your expenses again after making a well-thought-out budget plan. But this time, I want you to do it again in order to see if it actually works.

At this point, tracking your expenses shouldn't be too difficult anymore and should not feel too burdensome.

In the first month, using a new budget is the most important. By the end of the month, know what you think worked and what did not, and use that in making a new budget for the upcoming month. Honestly, it will probably take you about a couple of months before you sort out perfect budgeting. So, if you think that it didn't work for you the first time, don't give up just yet. Great money management may take some time and practice, so be patient and don't give up right away.

I don't think you need to track all your spending and expenses for the rest of your life, though. For many people I know, they recorded each of their expenses for months. When they already knew their budget as well as their spending habits, they stopped tracking their daily expenses regularly. This practice will surely give you a chance to develop a better sense of where you think you are at when it comes to spending, and when you are getting close to maxing out your set budget.

Breaking down of Budget by Percentage

What I learned is when you look at your budget by percentage, instead of numbers, it is going to be more convenient.

Here's the breakdown of my current budget:

Fixed Expenses: 32.89%

Variable Expenses: 46.02%

Remainder: 21.09%

But remember that we may have different incomes, so in order to look at and imitate what someone else spends is not going to benefit you. Ultimately, after calculating everything, I'd estimate that I'm roughly living on a little more than half of my income and the rest goes to short-term savings as well as a retirement plan.

As mentioned earlier, minimalist budgeting may not work the first time you do it. Actually, it did not work for me as well at first. I exceeded my budget plan for my first two months. That's when I knew I needed to change something in my approach. The following are the things I did in order to perform it successfully:

➤ I tried to avoid consumerism

This has been the first and most important step for you. Most of the time, it's so easy to set out the mind-set of buying or attaining more, to shop for pleasure or to relieve stress, or simply buying impulsively. This is a mind-set that roots from years of being exposed to advertising, and it's not easy to stop. You can start by becoming more aware of it and by telling yourself that you'll no longer find pleasure in getting and buying material things.

If ever you find yourself wanting to buy something so bad, sit back and take a deep breath. You can list it down and let days go by before buying it. Normally, the impulse will dispel. Think thoroughly about every purchase you make and ask yourself if you really need it or you can survive without it. Trying to live with a minimalist budget is trying to live only with things that are truly important and get joy from doing things.

➤ I saved up for rainy days

Before you reach financial peace of mind, it's important for you to have funds you can use for rainy days or times of emergency. Otherwise, you are always going to live on the edge, from pay check to pay check. Every unexpected spending that comes up will disrupt everything I'm recommending below.

You can get started here: Save up about $500 by putting aside $50 to $100 every time you get your pay check, and eventually build up to $1,000 or more.

In order to do this, cut out pointless expenses. Look carefully at the way you spend, including regular payments you may have forgotten about, and see what cut you can make. Some of these cuts may include the following:

- ❖ magazine subscriptions
- ❖ buying books (instead, borrow from libraries)
- ❖ cable TV
- ❖ more expensive mobile phone plan

- ❖ gourmet coffee

- ❖ a bigger home than you need

- ❖ storage space

- ❖ shopping for too much food

- ❖ too much entertainment that you can skip

Make the cut and put the money to you rainy-day funds. There shouldn't be a limit for how much you can save for this budget, but if you want, you can still have a limit of how much.

➢ I got out of debt

Debt payments aren't essential – well, you shouldn't have them in the first place anyway. However, until you have settled your debt payment, they are going to be a headache.

After saving at least $500 for your rainy-day fund, you can put off your extra income towards debt payment, one debt at a time, until you are all paid up. Perhaps put a bit on each pay check towards your rainy-day fund.

Last Piece of Advice

There's no shortcut in making a budget that you can stick to and that will work for you. A budget is, nevertheless, a breathable outline for your money habits. A budget shouldn't just reflect your present lifestyle but also be the main tool that is going to help you reach your bigger goals. On the other hand, if you already have all the things you might possibly need, then put aside that money for your emergency funds.

Other Important Things to Remember

Use it together with good budgeting tactics. You are able to use minimalism – and more mindful shopping habits – to make your budgeting skills better. However, practicing minimalism alone does not replace good budgeting methods. Figure out if you have enough self-control over your spending. Have you actually grasped the flow of money in your life? Do you have an idea where your money goes every month? These are important questions to answer when trying to improve your budget.

Learn how you can align minimalism with your long-term budget goals. Always look at the big picture. You want to ensure that you are also saving money for your future goals. It's important to make sure that your money is going to the right places; places where it will help you grow your wealth or get closer to where you want to be and what you want to have.

This just means that along with cutting down your expenses, you must also be putting your money on savvy savings and investments that match your long term and midterm goals. For example, if all your unspent funds are sitting in a no-yield checking account, you may consider moving them to a high-yield savings account, low-fee mutual fund, or certificate of deposit, depending on what your financial goals are.

Don't be afraid of your debt; instead, just be mindful about it. There are minimalists who preach absolute hatred towards debt, which includes student loans and mortgage debt. However, financial experts caution that there could be room for savvy debt management within your budget.

Yes, you must absolutely pay down high-interest credit card debt and think carefully before you take on new debt. However, the concept of leveraging money could be a really smart method to build your wealth. As long as you do it right, with the right kind of debt, you are good to go.

For example, getting the right amount of student loans, which could be an important investment for your career in the future – try to get no more than your expected first year's salary. Paying down a fairly low-interest mortgage aggressively might not make sense if you have more persistent financial goals, like putting up funds for your retirement savings account.

So, always think carefully before shunning all debt. These could be beneficial as long as you know how to manage them.

It's important to practice that same level of mindfulness in your financial life. As you reconsider your belongings to decide whether they add value to your life or you're better off without them, try the same practice with your financial accounts.

Do your retirement accounts still bring relevance to your life, or is it better for them to be rebalanced due to current economic and personal changes? Does your savings account still meet all the expenses you need to pay? Does the amount in your bank keep you happy and contented? Take a moment to reassess and re-examine the financial situation on which you rely so as to make your financial future happier.

Chapter 5

BUDGETING FOR THE LONG TERM

It seems that today, everyone has been talking about minimalism – it just has become a trend. From tiny houses to decluttering, to living with no more than a certain number of belongings, a minimalist lifestyle attracts people who are looking to change or improve something in their life. And as you know by now, minimalism is very beneficial for those who want to manage their budget on a long-term basis.

Budget to Your Heart's Content

Budgeting is the secret to saving money, regardless of what lifestyle you would like to have! By having a clear plan of you need and having a clear picture of the road to take, it's going to be easy for you to manage your budget as a minimalist in the long term.

Minimalist attitude is something we should have. This budget could also help you learn how to make the most of your budget, minimize your spending, and make your savings even bigger.

If you choose to ride a bike as your form of transportation to work, then you avoid spending on anything except for the bicycle itself, which you had probably paid for when you bought it, and its maintenance. If your mortgage or rent is a huge chunk of your money, maybe consider a smaller house, which means you might have to eliminate a lot of your "stuff" because you'll have limited room space. Even food could be minimized by growing vegetables and herbs, instead of buying them in store.

Follow Your Budget, or it is Pointless

How many of us have made a budget, followed it for a while, then ignored it completely? Pretty much almost every one of us! As mentioned earlier, it is not that simple to make the budget plan, and if we're feeling overwhelmed by it, looking at it again is something we are trying to avoid. But if you want better things to come, just follow it!

Spend at least 15 minutes every week to check your budget plan and make sure that you are on the right track. Yes, there are days when you will not be able to follow it. But it is okay; we're only human! But remember that the more we look at it, the easier it is for you to get used to it and for it to become a habit. Knowing that you can control your finance is super empowering and fulfilling. Just try it, and you will know what I mean!

Buy Things that Last

Of course, there are things that are only good for a while like food, clothing, etc. and that's alright. But there are many things that are meant to last for a long time. When you need to shop for something, you may want to focus on making sure that you're buying something that you can benefit from in the long run.

This might mean that you need to spend a little bit more money on it. The idea behind minimalist budgeting is not to avoid spending your money or being frugal but making the most of your money, whether it means you have to pay triple of the price of the cheaper version. Just imagine buying a microwave that costs $50 that would likely break down after a year of use, or even earlier. Do you think it's more worthy than its $150 version that comes with 5 years warranty? Invest in high-quality furniture, and you'll spend less as you wouldn't have to replace it every so often. It should always be quality over the price tag.

Choose What You Need, Not What You Want

If you don't know already... yes, there's a difference between what you need and what you want. It's so easy to get caught up in satisfying your desires for the latest gadgets or the nicest clothes. While these things are indeed necessary for day to day needs, they don't have to be the grandest things.

As I kept mentioning in the earlier part of this book, marketers love preying on people who are soft when it comes to persuasion, even leading us down the road of what they want you to buy. But with a minimalist mindset, you will be able to focus on what you need rather than what you want.

It's also worth noting that the things we own don't define *who* we are! While the way you wear clothes may reflect your personality, it doesn't really define what's inside you.

Budgeting as a minimalist for the long term is truly attainable, so it's truly worth a try. There's no denying that a lot of people are so used to not saving and getting by with the money they earn, overlooking the amount they are already spending on a normal day. This is why applying mindfulness in all aspects of our lives, including our financial life, is extremely important.

Chapter 6

SETTING YOUR FINANCIAL GOALS

Again, in case I haven't stressed it enough already: The intention behind minimalist budgeting is NOT to be more frugal but to eliminate excess spending on things that don't bring value to your life, or as Marie Kondo says it, "things that don't spark joy."

Setting your financial goals can be rather difficult, especially if you have not even mastered the basics of goal setting yet. While money seems to make many things twice as complicated for some, you don't have to worry; here are the tips that will help you set your financial goals successfully.

1: Be Realistic

No matter what kind of goal you are trying to set, it's very important to always be realistic. If you are earning a minimum wage and your goal is to save a million by the end of the month, that's not realistic.

I know I mentioned how you should dream big or set a big goal. But there should be a limit on how big your goal is. And if it's really your dream to earn a million, give a realistic timeline to yourself; otherwise, you are just putting stress on your life over something that is not practical with your current financial situation. And if that's the case, just how keen will you be to set your financial goal again and give it a try?

It's okay to start small. As soon as you reached that goal, you can make your way up to the bigger and greater goal eventually.

2: Decide Your Target

Of course, you must have a target amount as well as a target deadline. Be as specific as you can. When your goals are specific, you will have more chance to accomplish it earlier.

If you write that you want to be "rich", don't you think it's too vague? I mean, how rich do you want to be? Another thing I don't get is when people use the word "someday" too much. When is "someday" going to happen anyway?

When you don't commit to a number and a date, you're just giving yourself more reasons to fail or back out, even. And you're setting yourself to failure. If you are really serious about setting your financial goals, try to give your best.

3: Learn How to Budget

We've discussed this topic earlier, so I'm going to be brief on this one.

It is not only about choosing the number, it also has something to do with plotting your way to attain your main goal. And in all financial situations, budgeting plays a big part.

To successfully meet your set date and amount, learning how to add and subtract is essential. You must know which expenses must be maintained and which ones are to be eliminated.

Setting your financial goal should be easy as long as you follow the right path. Forget the people you know who weren't very successful in attaining their goals. Instead, focus on working hard and the possible outcome once you successfully reach your goal. There might be times when you feel tempted to change direction, but fight off those temptations and think of the reasons why you started all these things in the first place.

Chapter 7

DEALING WITH THAT DREADED DEBT

The day I had that realization that my old habits had floated up, I was at a mall with my wife, shopping for Christmas gifts. It was just a snap. I randomly had the question in my head that changed my life forever....

"Why do we have to give people new things to express our love to them?"

Sounds like a simple question, I know. But, why is that instead of taking them to the beach, spending time with them, giving them a hug, helping them with house chores... we give them gifts? Are material things more valuable than offering them our time? I mean at least money is something you can earn again, but time... it's something you can't take back. So, why does it seem like people would prefer to give their loved ones material gifts on special occasions?

If someone gave me a shirt for my birthday, would I really appreciate it more than if someone chose to invite me to go to the beach for that special day?

I realized that day that I should value time and experience more than materials things. The same day was the day I changed my spending habits forever. I no longer waste my time, energy, and space buying things that I know I don't need.

Minimalism is really about transformation.

If you choose to leave your possessions and turn yourself to the things that are more important, such as relationships, you are really committing to changing yourself.

You will then begin to see life differently and ask things from a different perspective.

That's what happened to me since that day at the mall. And I am extremely grateful to the universe for giving me this kind of realization I knew I needed.

Now, going back to the question... *how can minimalism help you get out of debt?*

Everyone wants to get out of debt – I mean who would want monthly responsibility of paying back money, right? Well, the first thing you need to know is that you can make this happen, probably earlier than expected.

According to a magazine I was reading the other day, a lot of people actually just accept that they're going to be in debt, one way or another, for the rest of their lives – at least in the US.

But wouldn't it feel amazing to never get bills in your mailbox again? Can you just imagine?! Well, minimalism can help you make this happen. Let's get this straight, though: there is no such thing as a get-out-of-debt card – changes are necessary in order to make this happen. And to do that, you have to manage your money better.

A lot of people are guilty of spending more than what they earn. Unfortunately, when you owe money to companies, you don't really own anything that you're paying them for. Just see everyone who fell in hard times and happened to lose their homes. The banks are the new owner of those properties now. Once you fall behind on your mortgage, it's only a matter of time until the bank grabs the keys from your hands.

Well, there are two things you can do about this.

First of all, you can cut your expenses, and the second thing is to find a way to increase the money that is coming in.

You're probably thinking, "If only it was that simple!" Well, sit down, relax, and think of all the things you spend your money on every single month. Make sure to include food, gourmet coffee, transportation, and monthly online subscriptions – not only the major bills you need to pay for. Now, list them all down and pick ones that you know you can live without.

The next step is to look at the things that might hurt when taken out, such as the internet, Netflix subscription, or eating out. Cut back to the basic internet and mobile phone plans and remove eating out completely and resort to just cooking at home. Prioritize the more important things. Some of the things you are regularly paying for are conveniences that you basically don't need to get by.

Next is to figure out how you can make more money in order for you to pay off the debt you have accumulated.

You can start by emptying out your home of stuff that you no longer use or need. If possible, sell them to add funds toward paying your bills.

For many, having a side business has been their solution. The same thing worked for me. I was working full-time when I started an online business. I managed to make it work, thankfully. Now, I've been self-employed for many years, and there's no way I'm going to look back.

If you know how to sort things according to their importance, making decisions on what you need and what you don't becomes easier. And getting my priorities straight is one of the best things I learned from living minimally.

7.1 Using the Concept of Minimalism to Plan Your Personal Transformation

I hope my story has encouraged you to take a step toward the transformation you need. Otherwise, I suggest you to start observing people when you are in public places. Observe their behaviour as they shop for more material things. Just observe the excitement registered on their face as they make the purchase and walk out from the store.

And then just imagine how they might feel on the day they have to pay their credit card bills.

Is their purchase still worth it?

I'm confident to say that most of the time, it's not. Most of the things we buy are not worth putting yourself in that sort of financial trouble.

There are more things in life that are more fulfilling.

Minimalism helps us see more important things and encourages us to ask questions about why we feel like we need to collect more and more things and what are the possible outcomes for these actions.

There are a lot of reasons why people spend too much and accumulate too many things. But one of the main reasons is to fulfil their unmet needs.

Of course, it's important to buy certain things such as food, clothing, and shelter to secure our safety. But if what you're looking for is freedom and happiness, shopping and splurging thousands of dollars in debt is not really the right path to attaining freedom and happiness.

The truth is that true freedom comes from financial stability and security, as well as the nurturing and cultivating of personal relationships. And while commercials will argue that "*you can't buy happiness, but you can buy ice cream; and that's kind of the same thing,*" YES. Buying ice cream indeed boosts your mood at the moment. But would it benefit you for a long time? And just for the sake of argument, let me tell you that while ice cream can make some people happy when consumed, think about how it will affect your health if you choose to eat ice cream often to fill that *void* in you.

One of the best things you can do for yourself is to figure out what really triggers you to shop too much and over accumulate. And then use the answers to understand why and how it has stolen your opportunity to attain genuine happiness.

Instead of shopping:

❖ Work on strengthening and finding loving and meaningful relationships with people around you.

❖ Learn to be appreciative toward things you already have.

❖ Follow what genuinely makes you happy and not what makes other people happy.

Money and possessions give us false happiness.

Always be curious about your real motivations and use what you find to bring your life towards the things that make you feel free from the possessions, pressures, and emptiness that materialism brings.

7.2 Mistakes to Avoid When Dealing With Debt

When you're already drowning in debts, it's so easy to feel confused as to what to do about it. While there are a lot of approaches you can do to ease your struggles when paying off your debts, here are the most common mistakes you should avoid when dealing with debt.

- **Ignoring the debts**

Ignoring your debt is one of the worst things you could do. By letting your bills pile up, you will just accumulate more dues in the form of late fees and interest. What's worse, you might even end up getting sued, have your car reclaimed, or if you're renting a house, get evicted. Regardless of how terrible it might make you feel, you have to settle those bills and return any calls you get from your creditors. And, of course, you must create a plan for how you are going to deal with those debts.

- **Dealing with debts without enough funds**

It's very just silly to think that you could get out of debt without having a budget in writing to help you manage your spending and overall money. The truth is that there's simply no tool that is more important to good debt management than proper budgeting. It is the only way to guarantee that the right amount of money goes towards paying off your top priority debts without compromising your daily needs.

- **Falling behind on your payment**

If you fail to keep up on your car loan, there is a big chance that your car will be reclaimed. And this could happen without warning or anything even if you just missed a single payment. Just imagine having your car one day and losing it on the next. This gets even worse if you need your car to go to work every day. This is not only going to be inconvenient for you but also for the people who depend on you if you have a family.

- **Paying Only Your Most Forceful Creditors**

If you have multiple debts and your money is tight, don't choose to pay the most aggressive creditor first just because you are intimidated. Don't be forced to pay the creditors that hound you the most. Look at them equally. If you know one debt is better settled first than the other, then do it.

- **Making Promises to Creditors That You Can't Keep**

When you're getting confronted by a creditor about a past-due debt or discussing how you are able to catch up on past-due payments, don't make promises that you know from the beginning you can't keep. It's important to make decisions derived from your budget and income and not on what your creditor wants to hear.

- **Refusing to Stop Using Your Credit Cards**

While this is a no-brainer, many people still commit this mistake. Keep in mind that if you are already having issues with your credit card payments, it's smart to put those credit cards away so that you are not racking up even more debt. If you are considering buying something and you currently don't have enough money to pay for it, just try to forget about that item completely. If you want to avoid temptation, then always leave your credit card at home and have just enough cash with you when you need to go out.

- **Taking Out a Loan against Your Home to Settle Your Debt**

If you are struggling just to survive and have equity in your home, it could be very appealing to get a loan and putting your house as collateral. However, using your home as collateral to acquire a second loan is one of the worst ideas you can come up with. You could eventually find yourself in a place where you could not pay for both loans and would lose most of your valuable assets.

- **Getting a Loan from a Non-Traditional Lender**

There are actually for-profit credit agencies that are going to persuade you into borrowing money from them for you to get through your financial woes. Also, companies like that will make you believe that they are going to help you pay your debt. Don't deal with these non-traditional lenders, especially the ones that will require you to use your valuable assets collateral. It's so tempting to get a loan from one of these lenders. Make sure to read your paperwork carefully, and it is likely that you will find that these loans are very expensive source of funds and that their terms are essentially designed, so you'll end up losing the properties you used as collaterals.

- **Choosing To Work With a For-Profit Credit Counselling Agency**

There's just no reason to work with a credit counselling agency that's for-profit. These agencies have one purpose only, and that is to make as much money as they can. Because of this, it's hard to trust their recommendations and believe them that they want the best for you. Actually, some of the for-profit credit counselling agencies might tell you to do stuff that earns them money at your expense and could essentially get you into legal trouble.

- **Asking a Friend or Relative to Co-Sign a Loan**

If you cannot get a loan from a traditional lender like a credit union or a bank due to your financial problems, think very carefully before asking a friend or family member to help by co-signing for a loan. This is not a good idea because if ever you fall behind your dues, they're going to run after the co-signee. This means you're not only making a problem with money but also with your relationships with people that care about you.

7.3 Effective Strategies to Clear Debts

No matter how much your debt is and how long you have been struggling with it, you have to know that there's always hope. Here are some tips you can follow to get out of debt from a minimalist perspective.

- **Get Professional Help**

You can find a financial advisor who can help you. Yes, this might cost you some money, but you can look at it as an investment. On top of telling you how you can manage your finances better, they could also save you a lot of time. The process might be quite slow, and it might span several months. However, you have to realize that you can't repay a big debt overnight. Thorough measures have to be taken over the course of time in order to control the damage you bring to your bank account and earn enough money to settle your debt.

- **Plan Your Expenses**

I understand that some people may be averse to hiring a professional financial advisor, especially the ones who can't really afford hiring one. But don't you worry, as anyone, even you, who don't have any financial background, can surely plan out his finances as long as he puts his mind to it. This might require you to take a seat and compute your numerous expenses, and you might even be required to narrow your expenses down to a day-to-day level. It's suggested that you assign a day-to-day spending cap, but don't sacrifice too much and just eat packet ramen for every meal. You might not be able to always experience luxury, but you definitely shouldn't need to live like a tramp just to get rid of your debt.

- **Don't Spend On Things You Don't Need**

I don't know how many times I have said this in this book already. But at this stage, you shouldn't be spending on things you don't need right now, even though you think it's something that you might need later in your life. It's easy to see why, but you'll be amazed that some people will still spend a lot of money on items they don't need. And the reason behind this is actually kind of saddening – some people do this because they've already lost a lot and feel that they can no longer rectify the situation. So, they might as well go all out and enjoy life as much as they can. This mind-set is very toxic. I really hope that you're determined in choosing the better way.

Chapter 8

VALUING TIME

Time is money. In fact, if you come to think of it, most of us don't only sell our skills to earn money, but also our time.

It might be a cliché you have heard many times before, but you know it's true. We may not receive the same opportunities in life, but we all get the same 24 hours in a day. Time is money, so we need to give value to time as we do to the money. In fact, treat it as more valuable because as I said earlier: money is something you can earn again, while time is something you cannot get back.

The idea of saying time is money opens up a whole range of relationships between our money and time. The time is possibly the easiest to theorize. Again, all of us have exactly 24 hours each day. What we don't have an idea about is when it is going to end. How we spend time highly depends on us. Money is a bit vaguer. Depending on where and when we were born, we start off in a given socio-economic situation. Then factors like opportunity and education all come in to shape us. All these, along with other bigger background factors such as current economic conditions at the time of our living, define to a great degree how much money we're going to have.

8.1 Time vs. Money

As humans, we are bound by two concepts, time and money. Every day, when we go to work, we're offering our time in exchange for money. Others have more money to buy other people's time. On the other hand, others choose to invest their money in order to make more and more money. No matter how you manage your time and money, you're falling into one of these categories:

No Time and No Money

A lot of employees fall into this category. There are people who have no control over their time because they are working. And at the same time, they don't generate enough money to become financially independent as they live pay check to pay check.

People under this category likely don't have any savings, so they will probably get bankrupt within a month or two after losing their job. These people don't have real financial stability and also very little time to enjoy their life.

No Time and a Lot of Money

People who are self-employed, professionals, as well as small business owners, generally fall into this category. They usually have more money than the previous category. However, they usually work twice the amount of time.

People in this category have extremely high stress levels and usually miss important occasions because their world revolves around only their work. Even though they have above-average income, they don't have a lot of time to spend outside of work.

A Lot of Time and No Money

People in this category are usually the ones who work part-time, are students, or those who live off social assistance. They generally have more time than the average small business owners or employees. The catch, however, is that they barely have money to enjoy their free time completely.

A Lot of Time and a Lot of Money

Those who fall within this category are the luckiest. The internet has opened a lot of doors to people that couldn't be enjoyed by many people decades ago. Most people who enjoy this lifestyle are those who work online and investors who have control over their time and their income. There are the lucky ones who enjoy true freedom from time and financial problems. Other people who may also fall under this category include actors, musicians, and writers who usually generate royalties for their works. Investing your time into things that are going to pay you bonuses over time helps you enjoy life with a lot of money and a lot of time.

If you are living in a developed nation, changing your lifestyle might be easier. However, even if this is that case, it will still take effort, determination, and planning to be successful at it.

8.2 How to Work Smarter Not Harder

Waking up at 5 o'clock in the morning every day, traveling for almost an hour to get to the workplace, spending 9 hours at the office, and getting paid for 8 was a norm to me a few years back. My father said to me, "Son, you should work smarter, not harder," as I called him one weekend complaining about how I was starting to hate my job.

How can we do this?

Here are some important ways of how you can work smarter rather than harder.

Plan your tasks before you even start them

Planning is one of the best ways to work smarter. Planning can be done before you go to bed at night. List down all the projects and tasks you need to do in the following days, weeks, or even months. After doing this, do a comprehensive review of each of the tasks, classify them based on their importance, and figure out how much time is needed to execute each item on the lists. This will make doing this a lot easier.

Learn how to delegate

Some things can just be too overwhelming to the point that you can no longer do them on your own. Delegating tasks to others would be the best solution for this. This method will effectively free up your schedule and allows you to do other things that are important.

Have strict deadlines and stick to them

There are major tasks that tend to be big and involving. Because of this characteristic, we're drawn to procrastinate and not to do them even if we could have done them earlier. This is a harmful habit. In order to work on such tasks in a smart way, just divide them into smaller, manageable tasks. And with that, you can work on them one at a time. By doing this, you can assure that you can focus on the tasks and you will end up with a high-quality result and of course, you will be able to finish them on time.

Learn to Manage Your Time Better

Time management is one of the critical skills you want to improve if you want to work smarter. Time management will help you assign specific periods of time to every task that you need to do. A part of time management is to learn how to eliminate all the distractions around you. This will allow you to focus more on the task at hand. Finally, avoid multitasking. People think that they are being productive when they multitasking, but it just gives an illusion that you're finishing more things when the truth is that you are just delaying the tasks.

Take a Break

Both your body and mind need a break, and this is a part of working smart instead of working hard. Working for too long can definitely wear you out and reduce your capacity to do the necessary tasks. This is one of the reasons why for some people, no matter how much they work, they still get little results from their hard work. Set at least 20 minutes of break throughout the day to freshen up your mind and recharge your energy. With a fresh mind and body, it is going to be easier for you to maximize the results of your hard work.

Working smart involves strategy and when done right, leads to high-quality work. Following the tips mentioned above can help you to change your working methods and make them even better. Not only will you accomplish more within a short period of time, but you'll also have higher levels of energy left by the end of the day.

8.3 Why Society Doesn't Value Time

Have you ever noticed how some people think that they have a lot of time to do whatever they want to do? And have you ever wondered why this is the case?

These are the same people who you usually find in situations where they need to ask you to lend a hand on a project or give them a hand to do something they claim to be very important. It's also very common to hear this popular line from them… "Don't they realize how much pressure I am under right now?"

If they only knew how to value time, they wouldn't get caught in this situation.

But the question is… why do some people don't value this non-renewable resource? It's simply because they have no idea how to value it. If you find yourself in this situation, then let me guide you about how you can/should value your precious time.

Remember: Life is too short to be wasted

What will you do when someone asks you to offer him 5 hours of your day in exchange of $20? Would you take it? If you love yourself, please say NO. The way you value time reflects how you value yourself. And you are worth more than that! You're worth being paid enough, so don't sell yourself short. You deserve all the gratitude you can get from offering someone your time.

Know your value and know how to treat yourself better. Keep in mind that you are worth more than just a few pennies.

Repeat that to yourself, actually, believe in it, and act like it! There is no other way to do this. While I can't really walk you through each step in the process, here are some tips you can follow so you can treat your time better to make the most of it.

Don't Be Late: Being late shows how you don't value not only your time but also of others.

Use Your Time Wisely: Every second is worthy. As much as possible, I try to stay occupied anywhere I am at any time. When I'm riding the subway, I would read books or the newspaper. I listen to podcasts when I'm in the shower. I read books until I fall asleep. I try to use my spare time for self-improvement, as long as it's convenient for me. For me, it's all about using every moment of the day in an efficient way.

Know Your Priorities: What are the important things you do? Scrolling down on social media and keeping updated with other people's lives? Browsing online to look for things to buy when you have work you have to finish? Learning how to prioritize is extremely important. Decide what matters most and do it first.

Avoid Making Excuses: Everyone hates this, yet many are guilty of this. Look, I know it doesn't feel good to be held up by traffic, which causes you being late and missing the meeting. But why didn't you leave home early enough to make it on time despite the traffic? Stop using any excuse to save you from your own mistake. Be responsible for your action and value your time as well as other people's time.

Size Doesn't Matter: No matter how big or small, everything makes a difference when working toward success, your objectives, or anything you want to achieve. Take your time to say thank you. Give your partner a kiss before leaving to work. Listen to the news while you are in the shower. Every little thing is important.

Concentrate on the Present: All the things you are doing right now are going to benefit you in the future. But if you don't give importance to the present, it's going to be easy for you to get stuck in the never-ending loop of *"I'll do it tomorrow."* But remember that tomorrow never comes; it's just another new version of today. So, do it now, and do your best.

Stop Procrastinating: This is probably the simplest yet the trickiest culprit for wasting a person's time. It's so easy to identify someone who is procrastinating, yet many people still don't do anything about. If you find yourself ignoring an important work-related task to read Facebook Newsfeed or scroll through your Instagram, then you have a problem, my friend.

Procrastination kills motivation, creativity, and it doesn't benefit you. Just step up, get rid of all the distractions that trigger procrastination, and do what you need to do. If you find this difficult, just think like this: When you focus on doing your job, you will be able to finish it early; you will have more time to do the things that distract you without feeling guilty for doing it.

Take Control: This is probably the most important one, so read this carefully. Your problems are your problems, so no one else but yourself has to be responsible and accountable for it. By letting someone else affect your life and take that control, you are making a big mistake. Make better choices. Your life, your rules. You do you. If you fail at something, it is okay – just try again until you become successful at it. Believe in yourself and believe what you are capable of. Never let other people degrade you or make you feel insignificant. Only your judgment is important.

8.4 Busy vs. Productive

Day after day, it seems like the society and its people are becoming busier and busier than ever – which is kind of ironic as we are progressively creating new technologies that are supposed to give us convenience. Today, it seems like no one can find "free time" to do anything. It's a norm to run late for meetings, grab a meal on the go, and spend extra time at work. It's just so hard to keep up.

The most efficient and productive people are the ones who know how to own their day. They work hard in maximizing their time in order to be as productive as possible, not just to be occupied to do something.

The quest to be more efficient at work has emerged from the misconceptions about what having a productive workday really is. It has also made many people think that being busy is equivalent to being productive.

But the truth is that there is a huge difference between being busy and being productive. I spent years saying "yes" to all the opportunities that came my way and occupying myself with things that I can barely handle. But fortunately, I got to a point where I broke up my relationship to being busy and was able to introduce myself to being productive.

The Difference between Busy and Productive

Busy People	Productive People
Want to look like they have a mission	Always have a mission
Have many priorities	Have few priorities
Say yes quickly	Think hard before saying yes
Focus on action	Focus on clarity before action
Keep all doors open	Limit access to their doors
Talk about how busy they are	Let their results do the talking
Talk about how little time they have	Make time for important things
Aim for multitasking	Focus on one thing at a time
Make rushed decisions	Take their time for quality results
Always talk about wanting to change	Make necessary changes

Benefits of Stopping Being Busy and Becoming Productive

When you finally break up your toxic relationship with being busy, here are the benefits you will be able to reap:

You will make better projects. You will have enough time to create project-based learning unit plans and resources since you will no longer spend a crazy amount of time doing a simple task.

You will be inspired to take creative risks. When you find the root cause of working too much, you will be inspired to do things you didn't imagine you were capable of. Because you will have more time for yourself when you are productive, you will be able to have enough time to focus on your passion.

Your important skills will be improved. You will be able to figure out the skills you want to focus on. You will learn the things you are really good at and will have the chance to improve them if you choose to.

You will learn the importance of clarity. Productivity leads to clarity, the bluntness of expression, and purpose. It improves your ability to have a clear description of what has to be done, why it's important to do it, and how you can do it right.

You will have a work-life balance. The most important benefit of being productive is that you will have more time in your hands to do other things you personally enjoy. You can attain work-life balance when you're clear about your goal and know how to stay focused on things you need to do. This abolishes the pointless activity that gives you stress and causes fatigue. Furthermore, it will give you more time to do things you truly enjoy.

8.5 Productivity and Minimalism

One thing that many people don't realize is how minimalism plays a big part in our productivity. A study published by Microsoft Canada in 2015 concludes the following:

Canadians' ability to filter out distractions is a function of their surroundings, not their demographics, media consumption, social media use, or device usage. People with higher selective attention appear to actively choose to have fewer distractions and multi-screen less frequency.

This means that one of the differences between people who can keep attention longer and others who can't is that they intentionally generate a setting with fewer distractions.

The connection the study is talking about is not that complicated to understand. This just means that less use of gadgets, less noise in your environment, fewer tasks you commit yourself into, and less multitasking you do, cannot only initiate faster results but also better results.

What many people don't realize, however, is that productivity shouldn't be measured by the *quantity* of work you finished but the level of *quality* you achieved carrying out a task. The metric is no way centered on speed of production, but the level of quality.

The metric to assess the level of your productivity isn't how many things you did within the given time; it is how well you did in the process.

I believe that a minimalist approach to productivity is important to generate a helpful environment for better focus.

This includes:

- ❖ **Uninstalling all social media apps on your phone.** If you're really dying to check other people's lives on social media, then make it a little more inconvenient by using your mobile browser or use your computer. Perhaps, that little inconvenience makes you feel uninterested in checking social media accounts anymore.

- ❖ **Turning off the notifications on your phone.** Unless you are waiting for an important call or text, it's best to turn off your phone's notifications for when you receive calls, texts, or any alerts from any apps on your phone.

- ❖ **Using a small paper as your to-do list.** It's just that when you have a bigger paper to use or unlimited space on your app to create a to-do list, it's so satisfying to fill it up with tasks. So, the use of a small paper that can hold all the most important to-do lists would be a great option.

- ❖ **Disconnecting the internet when it's not needed for work.** It's just so easy to click on your browser and check out something for a few minutes. But most of the time, those " few minutes" turn into hours of time being wasted.

- ❖ **Listening to calming music.** Whenever I work, I become more focused when I'm listening to instrumental music, while for some, classical music or just white noise works better.

- ❖ **Cleaning your workspace**. Clutter and too much stuff around us can be so distracting. So, before working, cleaning your surrounding beforehand would be a good idea.

Since I am either writing or running my business almost every day, these simple strategies have helped me improve the overall quality of my life: I plan fewer daily activities, I learned not to care much about social media, and I learned many things that I truly enjoy outside the internet.

The spill-over effect of using a minimalist approach to improve my productivity has blessed me with a delightful surprise and has led me to reap the benefits of minimalistic lifestyle more seriously. It keeps reminding me that a state of overwhelm is mainly self-induced and could easily be managed through self-control.

Conclusion

Minimize, minimize, minimize.

We live in a world that can be so complicated. We are always so busy in a world that is so noisy and very distracting.

In order to counter that overwhelmed feeling, there is a movement happening in today's age, which persuades the idea of living a minimalistic lifestyle.

This might mean living with less, buying less, and owning less. Learning how to give importance to quality over quantity is one of the best things you could do with your money. Yes, it might be hard at first, but once you learn the benefits, it will come naturally.

Yes, I put up this book sounding like I know everything about managing your budget with minimalism. However, keep in mind that just like you, I had never really learned how to manage my budget before. It was pretty difficult to manage my funds. One important

thing to remember is that it didn't happen overnight –
I spent countless hours to successfully master what I
preach. It was a process full of trials and errors.

I hope that this book has been helpful and gives you an
idea of how to manage not only your budget but also
your time. Furthermore, I hope this book encouraged
you to take a step back and evaluate what you really need
to live a rewarding life; you can spend considerably less.

Minimalism is not a synonym to being cheap – you
don't have to count pennies or deprive yourself of
necessities in order to create more wealth. Rather,
eliminating your excessive spending helps you have
more money to spend on things that matter more.

In my case, following a minimalist lifestyle has greatly
liberated my funds, which I can use for following my
dreams and fulfilling my goals. At the end of the day,
my best source of wealth hasn't been measured in
currency, but rather in the time and opportunity that I
now enjoy living with a lifestyle that I genuinely love.

www.ingramcontent.com/pod-product-compliance
Lightning Source LLC
Chambersburg PA
CBHW030522210326
41597CB00013B/1000